CW0055859

ANCIENT PLACES

The angels keep their ancient places;
Turn but a stone, and start a wing!
'Tis ye, 'tis your estrangèd faces
That miss the many-splendoured thing.

Francis Thompson, *The Kingdom of God*

To Ruth, to Fenn and May, and to Nicola, Annette and Susi

ANCIENT PLACES

The prehistoric and Celtic sites of Britain

Glyn Daniel and Paul Bahn
Photographs by Anthony Gascoigne

Constable · London

First published in Great Britain 1987
by Constable and Company Limited
10 Orange Street London WC2H 7EG
Foreword copyright © 1987 by Glyn Daniel
Introduction copyright © 1987
by Glyn Daniel and Paul Bahn
Illustrations copyright © 1987 by Anthony Gascoigne
Set in Monophoto Photina 10pt and
Printed in Great Britain by
BAS Printers Limited, Over Wallop, Hampshire

British Library CIP data
Daniel, Glyn
Ancient places: the prehistoric
and Celtic sites of Britain
1. Man, Prehistoric – Great Britain
2. Great Britain – Antiquities, Celtic
3. Great Britain – Antiquities
I. Title II. Bahn, Paul G.
III. Gascoigne, Anthony
936.1   DA90

ISBN 0 09 467210 5

CONTENTS

ACKNOWLEDGEMENTS

We would like to thank Andrew Best for his part in conceiving this project, and his help in bringing it to fruition. We would also like to thank Christina Gascoigne and Olivia Brett for their 'spotting' skills. Finally, we have to record that Glyn Daniel died on 13 December 1986 before this book went to press and only shortly after he published his memoirs, *Some small harvest* (Thames & Hudson, 1986). He ends his memoirs with the story of how his father, John Daniel, came to carry in his wallet a precept for his own life, and we print this below in Glyn's memory.

GLYN EDMUND DANIEL
1914–1986

Pray God that when I go there will
be some record of something done:
some small harvest reaped.

John Daniel

PAUL BAHN AND ANTHONY GASCOIGNE

FOREWORD

IT IS a pleasure and a privilege to write a foreword to this lovely book of photographs taken by Anthony Gascoigne, and to have been associated with Dr Paul Bahn in the selection of ancient places to be photographed. All the sites and monuments in this book date from pre-Roman times, a period of four millennia from 4000 BC to the Roman Conquest of Britain – a time over twice as long as the centuries that separate us today from the departure of the legions in the fourth century. All the ancient places here described have one thing in common: they come from age-old centuries unilluminated by any written or epigraphic sources. These are monuments of prehistoric and preliterate Britain, and while the archaeologist can find out much about their dates, often their original purpose is still unknown and mysterious.

When the Romans conquered Britain they found it occupied by a collection of tribes all speaking a Celtic language which was described as Ancient British and was the ancestor of modern Welsh and Cornish. This language originated in Central Europe and Gaul; when the first Celtic speakers arrived in Britain is difficult to assess accurately, but must have been early in the first millennium BC. The great hillforts like Maiden Castle, Barbury and Uffington Castle and the curious hill-figures such as the White Horse near Uffington and the Giant at Cerne Abbas are works of pre-Roman Celts.

The other great monuments in this book, the megalithic chambers, rows and circles, are pre-Celtic. They belong to the Neolithic Age of the archaeologists and were built before man knew the use of metal. Some of the chambers were tombs, others not. The only reasonable explanation of the stone circles from small ones like Scorhill in Devon to the great ones of Avebury and Stonehenge is that they were tribal centres, places of secular and ritual assembly. That the megalith builders were concerned with the sun is beyond dispute: Stonehenge is built to face the midsummer sunrise. According to Latin written sources the Celts had in their society a class of learned men and priests called Druids: the megalithic monuments were built in pre-Celtic times but the Celtic Druids could later have used them as temples.

Archaeologists are often mealy-mouthed about the beauties of their subject. They dig and date but never stand and stare. Yet many of our ancient stone circles have a breath-taking beauty and the excellent photographs in this book – some of them even with a character and quality of a Turner or Constable – convey this to us. They make me want to go back as soon as I can to the cold prehistoric beauty of the stone circles of Orkney and Cumbria so admirably portrayed here.

GLYN DANIEL

1 Arbor Low
2 Avebury
3 Barbury Castle
4 Callanish
5 Castlerigg
6 Cerne Abbas
7 Devil's Arrows
8 Duloe
9 Dun Carloway
10 The Hurlers
11 Knowlton
12 Lanyon Quoit
13 Long Stone
14 Long House
15 Maiden Castle
16 Merry Maidens
17 Nine Stones
18 Pentre Ifan
19 Ring of Brodgar
20 Rollright Stones
21 Rudston
22 Scorhill
23 Silbury Hill
24 Skara Brae
25 St Lythans
26 Stenness
27 Stonehenge
28 Swinside
29 Trethevy Quoit
30 Uffington hillfort
31 Uffington hill-figure
32 Wayland's Smithy
33 West Kennet

INTRODUCTION

PREHISTORIC SITES, by definition, are those for which we have no written evidence to give us a clue about their date and function. Only archaeological excavation and inference can provide information of this sort; and since archaeology is a relatively new subject, there have been centuries, and in some cases thousands of years, for myths and legends to arise about these mute relics of a remote age. The folklore of prehistoric sites abounds in witches, devils, giants and golden treasures; these charming fairy-tales not only explained the presence of huge stones or of enormous earthworks, but also often conveyed a moral message: hence many stone circles were said to be people turned to stone, usually for having continued their revelries past Saturday night into God's holy day, or simply for enjoying themselves on a Sunday!

One would think that in our supposedly secular, rational age, when we have ample solid archaeological evidence about these sites, the fairy-stories would cease to appear; but on the contrary, they continue to arise, though in a new, pseudo-scientific guise: since few people can now believe in giants and fairies, we are presented with ley lines, points of abnormal geomagnetic strength, computers for predicting eclipses, and so forth.

Much of this sort of nonsense arose in that bizarre period, the 1960s, when the younger generation, turning away from the more traditional religions, found itself in need of something to believe in, to cling to, to provide some reassurance that life was not a meaningless absurdity. There were two principal new schools of thought about the past, more or less diametrically opposed. The first, born of the Space Age, was inspired largely by Arthur C. Clarke's *2001: A Space Odyssey* – and particularly by Stanley Kubrick's powerful film of the book – to believe that all major human advances were triggered by some far more advanced culture somewhere in outer space, which turned up sporadically in the course of human development to nudge us in the right direction. In Clarke's fantasy, the manifestation of the alien presence was a mysterious monolith, a huge symmetrical slab of stone.

This comforting belief that 'we are not alone' was taken to extremes by the bizarre books of Erich von Däniken and others, which put forward the view that our ancestors had accomplished nothing by themselves, and that any relic from the past which appeared spectacular or difficult to achieve had actually been produced by – or under the direct tutelage of – visiting astronauts from other, far more advanced worlds. How could primitive, ignorant humans have built the pyramids or transported the Easter Island statues without extraterrestrial help? Needless to say, there is not a shred of concrete evidence for visits by alien astronauts, and this view of our ancestors' capabilities is highly insulting to their memory.

The other view, totally different, was that our ancestors themselves had all kinds of weird and wonderful knowledge and powers which for some reason we have since lost or forgotten. It is this kind of wishful thinking that lies behind the terribly earnest efforts of those trying to prove that stone circles were erected at spots where the earth's energy could be tapped, or that prehistoric, and indeed historic, monuments are strung out along lines of geomagnetic force. There have even been suggestions that prehistoric people could move and erect huge stones because they knew how to defy gravity! However, the idea that our ancestors needed powers of this sort to accomplish what they did is just as insulting as the spaceman theory. But if the Chariots of the Gods have crashed, and the Earth Magic is an illusion, what are we left with? Simply, human beings – with all their patience, ingenuity, stubbornness, and occasional fanaticism. This is not to deny that something like geomancy – divination by figures drawn on the earth – may have been a factor in the location of some sites; we know, for example, that many tombs in Imperial China were carefully placed according to the specifications of geomancers. But this is known from writings; and in any case, the prehistoric environment must have been full of intangibles – 'good' and 'bad places', rivers, hills, sacred or ancestral areas, and benevolent or malevolent spirits – of great importance to the monument builders, but for ever unknown to us.

Many prehistoric monuments, including some of those in this book, look so impressive because of the size and weight of their stones, or the fact that huge stones were lifted and placed on top of others, or that vast quantities of earth and rubble were dug out and piled up. Our wonder is enhanced by the knowledge that the builders had no bulldozers, no tractors, no drills. But it is the very fact that today we rely on such machinery so totally that can blind us to what life was like not so very long ago. Before gas or electric light, people rose early and retired early; before bicycles and motorised transport, people thought nothing of walking or riding very considerable distances; and before the artificial aids mentioned above, people accomplished remarkable feats of engineering with simple tools, rollers, pulleys and patience.

We therefore have a tendency to overestimate the difficulties involved in accomplishing tasks without our modern devices. Yet all trades have their specialists and their knacks. One has only to watch professional furniture removers handling grand pianos or wardrobes, or see quarrymen in Carreara, Italy, moving large lumps of marble, to realise that most megalithic monuments – aside from the few with really huge stones – would not have posed major difficulties to patient people used to working with them. This is not meant to imply that prehistoric specialists in megalithic architecture made a living simply by travelling the country, putting up monuments wherever they were paid to do so, or by supplying stones of requested size much like Obelix in the Asterix stories. On the contrary, we are stressing that putting up a small or medium-sized megalithic monument cannot have been an insuperable problem for any group of prehistoric farmers.

Indeed, the principal difference between our age and theirs may be that they had ample time to devote to their pet projects, while modern life has to be lived to a tight and merciless schedule. A glimpse of these earlier conditions can still be found in rural areas of South America, Africa or Asia, where animals are still the main means of

transport, and where people seem content to spend vast amounts of time on tasks which we would find stultifyingly dull. They have nothing else to do, nowhere to go in the evening, no television to stare at. Little wonder, then, that in times when British life was like this, people attached enormous importance to the gatherings, rituals, ceremonies and communal projects which broke the monotony. Most of our prehistoric monuments are probably the residue of such 'special activities'.

The earliest great stone monuments in Britain might have been built about 4000 BC; there were earlier ones in neighbouring Brittany. There is no evidence that any megaliths were built after the end of the second millennium BC. We must think of at least two thousand years of our prehistoric past occupied by the builders and users of these great stone monuments.

What happened to these sites after about 1000 BC? They may have been used for ritual and social purposes by the Late Bronze Age and early Iron Age inhabitants of Britain in the thousand years before the Roman Conquest. We know from classical writers like Julius Caesar and Tacitus that the pre-Roman Celtic inhabitants of Britain and Gaul had a society which included a special class or caste called *Druides* responsible for the religious, juridical and administrative life of the Celtic tribes. They could have celebrated their religious rites or had their secular meetings in stone circles. However, there is no archaeological evidence of this at all, and what we know of the religion of the Celts of northwestern Europe from classical writers suggests that the Druids worshipped and sacrificed in groves.

But what is clear is that the sacred and special nature of megaliths survived into Roman and post-Roman times: indeed, the importance attached to British prehistoric monuments by later people cannot be overemphasised. Long after the makers and the precise function were forgotten, people regularly cleaned the white chalk-figures on the hillsides, or gathered at the stone circles for festivities on certain days of the year. Beliefs attached to some monuments, to particular stones or to springs were so strong and durable that the early councils of the Christian Church discussed them at length; at first, the Church forbade such practices, but then, in its wisdom, it tried to incorporate these ancient and pagan faiths by 'Christianising' the beliefs or the monuments – this was done in many ways: crosses were placed on menhirs, and in Brittany, Central France, Spain and Portugal megalithic chambers were incorporated into Christian churches. In England, some churches were built beside monuments (cf. Rudston, page 123); the village of Avebury – but not the church – is partly inside the great prehistoric stone circle (Pages 21–43). At Knowlton in Dorset (Page 79) we have a church inside a henge monument. The church was not built until the twelfth century and it is well outside the village. Were the elder pre-Christian faiths of the megalith builders still affecting ordinary people in Dorset in the Middle Ages?

Similarly, it is no accident that Christianity features water rituals, such as baptism, using holy water as a symbol of life and purification; fire rituals (the lighting of the Paschal candle, the use of ash on Ash Wednesday); and of course seasonal rituals – Christmas Day was fixed on the feast of *Sol invictus*, the unconquered Sun. It therefore celebrates the birth of the god after the winter solstice, on the day when the sun starts its rise towards the spring; Easter, on the other hand, is still fixed on the first Sunday (day of the sun) after the first full moon after the spring equinox, the day when the sun triumphs over darkness and days are again growing longer than nights. Even the humble Easter Egg is a relic of the Orphic mystery religion, a symbol of the birth of a new world.

It is highly probable that beliefs of this sort also played a major role in the religious life of the builders and users of our prehistoric monuments. The Neolithic societies who constructed these great monuments were naturally affected by the seasons, and their gatherings in the circles were most probably for religious and ritual reasons – but we suspect they were also social and economic gatherings, and are constantly reminded of the Breton *pardons* (one of which is held in the stone rows of Carnac) which include cattle and hiring fairs as well as religious ceremonies.

Antiquaries like John Aubrey and William Stukeley ascribed our great stone monuments to the Ancient Britons and their Druidic priests. The Druids' supposed links with these monuments were discredited in the nineteenth century by archaeologists, but neo-Druid organisations arose, alleging that they had continuing existence from early Iron Age times, and demanding to celebrate the midsummer sunrise at Stonehenge; they were allowed to do this for several years by the Ministry of Works. Of course, they had no relation with the original Druids; and in any case, as we have said, the original Druids had no certain, or any, relationship with Stonehenge. This has not stopped the bogus Druids performing or demanding to perform their special ceremonies at the monument. They are an inoffensive lunatic fringe-gang, and provide us every year with amusing pictures of themselves in their white nighties walking down Primrose Hill, or robed in the sanctuary at Stonehenge. What is alarming is that Stonehenge has been adopted as a symbol by off-groups in modern England: among them those self-styled hippies that have occupied huge midsummer camps around the site in recent years, and done considerable damage in the process. In the last few years the Druids and the hippies have been banned from Stonehenge, and quite rightly. But why did the problem ever exist? Is it that the magic and mystery of Stonehenge and Avebury and other sites are compelling not only to dotty Druids but to a wide range of half-educated nomads who look for a faith that is not established?

During the 1960s and 1970s there arose a view that precise astronomical observations were also a major factor in the location and construction of many megalithic monuments. This idea was not unconnected to the ideas mentioned earlier, of the Space Age and of Earth Magic. In any case, it implied that our ancestors were not merely sophisticated but far more sophisticated than archaeological evidence had hitherto suggested. A campaign of precise measurement was pursued at many sites, a task made somewhat difficult and indeed subjective by their generally dilapidated condition, by the size and irregularity of the stones, and by the fact that many stones were broken, displaced or absent. Nevertheless, the claim was made that Stonehenge had been an accurate eclipse-predictor, and that many other circles and monuments were carefully and purposely aligned on a number of heavenly bodies and constellations, that an advanced stage of geometry had been involved in the construction, and even that an elite sect of 'mathematician–priests', using a special type of pottery, had run these sites and wielded power through them!

For some time, archaeologists were unable to muster an effective answer to the claims about astronomy and geometry, since very few of them were sufficiently numerate to understand or assess the mathematics and calculations involved. In recent years, however, some archaeologists, as well as astronomers and mathematicians with a grounding in archaeology, have examined the claims critically and concluded that they were in most cases exaggerated, and in many actually mistaken, either through ignorance of the archaeological evidence, or through ambiguous, imperfect or subjective recording of sites. These are not, we think, primarily astronomical observatories, though they may in a general way have been sun-oriented: it is possible that certain monuments had some simple solar and/or lunar alignments – Stonehenge, for example, *may* have been purposely aligned on the midsummer sunrise; and the sun breaks in to the inner chamber at Newgrange at dawn on the winter solstice. However, the claims for alignments on other heavenly bodies and obscure constellations are almost certainly invalid; there are so many things in the night sky that – quite by chance – *any* stone circle will incorporate alignments on some of them. Once again, as happens so often in archaeology, the earlier interpretations were based as much on wishful thinking as on hard evidence.

This phenomenon also occurs in the area of social archaeology, where there is a fierce determination to recover the unrecoverable – i.e. the social structures, kinship patterns, hierarchies and religious beliefs of vanished prehistoric peoples. In the last twenty years or so a large number of archaeologists – primarily, though not exclusively, in the New World – have begun to grapple with such problems, apparently believing that they can reconstruct past social life simply because they want to do so. But the evidence is not there. Of course, some deductions are possible at a very simple level – for example, rich or monumental graves versus small and poor ones; large, rich houses as opposed to humble huts. But it is naive to apply our western twentieth-century norms to prehistoric cases. We know from anthropological studies around the globe that human societies are so varied that a wide range of explanations may be applicable to the prehistoric data. Certainly, in many societies, the emperors, kings, nobles, chiefs and suchlike receive the kind of rich, spectacular tombs which we know from Egypt or China; but in Saudi Arabia, the fabulously wealthy kings are buried with no possessions in unmarked graves! In some societies the rich receive poor burials, while the poor receive rich grave-goods; in others, the rich graves are reserved for twins, or people who die of certain illnesses, or particularly holy people; or the rich may be cremated and scattered, while the poor are buried. The possibilities are enormously varied.

Similarly, rich monumental graves *may* contain a chief or king – but many are multiple tombs, and examples are known around the world of relatively egalitarian peoples spending a great deal of time and effort on building spectacular tombs for their community while living in comparative poverty; death is perceived as lasting longer than life, and so the community's wealth is poured into the tomb construction. Attempts to reconstruct prehistoric social life, therefore, can only start from archaeological evidence and may achieve a degree of probability – but they can never proceed very far without resorting to speculative 'Just-so stories' and eventually to pure guesswork.

In the same way, it is very difficult to learn anything about prehistoric rituals and religion, beyond the basic points that water, fire, the sun and moon, the seasons, and initiations and other transition rituals were almost certainly involved. There is an old saying that any object or feature the archaeologist cannot explain is labelled 'ritual', but there is a lot of truth in the jest. In fact, there is not a single prehistoric site which can be called 'religious' with absolute certainty. Sites like Stonehenge, Avebury and all the other stone circles and henges are assumed to have been centres for ritual and ceremony, and few if any archaeologists would question this interpretation, but we have to accept that it is a chosen interpretation, not an indubitable fact, as, for example, in the case of Egyptian or Greek temples where we have written evidence of the buildings' functions and of the rituals performed there.

And if the precise function of henges and circles is unclear, the situation is far worse for monuments such as the cursuses – long, parallel pairs of banks and ditches, named by Stukeley who thought they might be race-tracks – or Silbury Hill, where there are no artifactual remains to provide clues. Excavations of these monuments have enabled us to date them accurately, to assess the techniques of construction and even reconstruct the contemporary environment; but the rich burial many hoped to find in Silbury Hill has never been located, and it now seems likely that the tumulus is not a tomb but simply the biggest man-made prehistoric mound in Europe. We may never know its function but it is dramatic evidence of what our ancestors could achieve with simple tools.

It should be noted that the notion of 'our ancestors' producing their own monuments is a relatively new one in archaeology, for until the 1960s the dominant form of explanation in the subject was diffusionism: i.e. skills and innovations were usually thought to have been introduced to a region from a more advanced culture elsewhere. This view was less extreme than the 'spaceman theory', since it ascribed all developments to human beings, but it nevertheless constituted a kind of archaeological 'racism' by assuming that inventions, skills and the accompanying technology had all come to barbarian Europe, for example, from the enlightened, civilised regions of the Middle East and Greece.

There has understandably been endless speculation about the origins of the great stone monuments which figure often in the photographs in this book. Monuments similar in architectural design and construction are to be found in France, Spain and Portugal, north Holland and Germany and in southern Scandinavia, particularly Denmark. Were they all connected, the work perhaps of an ancient megalithic people or race? There has often been talk of the megalith builders of Europe and they have been thought of as separate from the earlier Neolithic people. For several decades it seemed correct to assume that

many aspects of the European Neolithic and Bronze Age, and particularly the use of gold, the megalithic monuments, and Stonehenge above all, should be ascribed to the influence and indeed the direct teaching of 'megalithic missionaries', colonists, metal traders or 'travelling undertakers' – all these views have been canvassed – from the eastern Mediterranean. The faience beads and bone sceptre mounts, the amber jewellery and the goldwork of the Wessex tombs, combined with the 'Cyclopean' stones and the 'Mycenaean' dagger carvings at Stonehenge (below) made it seem almost certain that Bronze Age Greece played an important role in Bronze Age Britain. But was this the case?

One distinguished scientist, though not an archaeologist, who thought he knew the answer was Sir Grafton Elliot Smith, successively professor of anatomy in Cairo, Manchester and London. He set out his views from 1911 onwards that all civilisations originated in Egypt and that the European megaliths were poor copies of Egyptian tombs. He specifically declared that the chambered long-barrows of southern England were barbarian copies of the *mastabas* of Ancient Egypt.

His Egyptocentric diffusionist views were only popular for a short while: his parallels were unconvincing, and no Egyptian artifacts of any kind have ever been found in any of the European great stone monuments. But the idea of a Near Eastern or east Mediterranean origin for the European megaliths, which had first been set out by Danish and Swedish archaeologists in the nineteenth century, persisted, and in the period 1925 to 1945 it was convincingly argued by archaeologists like V. Gordon Childe and others that it was people from the islands of the Aegean – the Cyclades and Crete – who diffused the idea of building megaliths and with it the religion of the Great Mother Goddess to western and northern Europe.

This attractive and well-argued thesis was shown to be no longer tenable when the developments of absolute dating by the radiocarbon method revealed that many of the megaliths of Brittany, Ireland and England were earlier than their supposed prototypes in the east Mediterranean. It is now clear that megalithic architecture began, independent of any Egyptian or Aegean stimulus, in many places in Europe and as early as the fifth millennium BC. How many independent centres there were we can still argue about, but certainly Malta, southern Spain and Portugal, Brittany, Denmark, Ireland and Britain. It is a fascinating subject for speculation and discussion why so many Neolithic societies in Europe translated their wooden and turf-built tombs into megalithic chambers.

However, the discovery that the diffusionist ties between barbarian Europe and the civilised east were illusory led to the development of an equally extreme and opposite view: that of independent invention of virtually everything. The Europeans were seen as cultural and technological pioneers in their own right, doing their own thing independently of, and often earlier than, their civilised neighbours.

As usual in archaeology, the truth probably lies between the two views, and prehistoric Europe – like any region other than remote islands – must

have developed ideas and techniques of its own, *and* received or modified others from neighbouring areas, including Greece and the Near East. After all, raw materials were already moving hundreds of miles during the late Ice Age, so that by the comparatively modern times with which we are concerned here (2000 or 3000 years BC) long-distance trading and contacts with other cultures, both nearby and remote, both overland and by sea, must have been a very common occurrence.

As a result, neighbouring countries have prehistoric monuments which are interrelated, and yet each region has unique features. Britain is certainly a good example of this phenomenon: we can be quite certain that the great stone circles are a British invention. Nothing like them exists in Europe. In Neolithic Britain the earlier wooden henge monuments were transformed into stone, a tradition reaching its triumphant success in Stonehenge – the work of some eccentric, eclectic and visionary chieftain–priest–architect whose name we shall never know. The monument is one of a kind; and it is gratifying that measures are at last being taken to improve the facilities for public viewing and visits.

The British, like most nations, take a keen interest in their history and in their archaeological heritage – witness the popularity of archaeological books and TV programmes, or the many people who visit excavations in progress – and Britain has produced many of the earliest and greatest practitioners of archaeology. Yet in some areas we lag far behind other countries: for example, we still lack a good, popular magazine about world archaeology, filled with colour photographs; and our Post Office has completely ignored our archaeological heritage as a source of illustrations for its stamps, unlike other countries where monuments and objects are depicted on some of the finest issues. We have had skulls of fossil men on a Darwin stamp in 1982, and a cromlech can be seen in the background of a 1984 stamp depicting an Irish cow (!), but the glories of our own archaeological heritage remain completely untapped.

In terms of books, the British are already well provided with guides, gazetteers of sites and general introductions to their archaeology; but there are very few publications whose illustrations are of really outstanding quality. In this volume we have had the opportunity to work with a photographer of the very highest calibre. The three dozen or so sites, presented with descriptive captions, were chosen for their visual impact, and we feel that Anthony Gascoigne's remarkable pictures help to reveal the character and atmosphere of the sites – the closest thing available to a three-dimensional effect!

GLYN DANIEL AND PAUL BAHN

ARBOR LOW

The Neolithic/early Bronze Age henge monument of Arbor Low, known as the 'Stonehenge of Derbyshire', stands in a dominant position with tremendous views. The oval bank is still high, and contains boulders weighing up to a ton; it encloses a ditch dug almost 2 m into the solid limestone – the removal of these 1500 cubic metres of stone (4000 tons) would have required fifty people to labour for six months. The henge contains an egg-shaped ring of fifty blocks of white limestone, all now recumbent and resembling the marks on a clockface; there is no proof that the stones ever stood upright – if they did so, they probably fell because of the extreme shallowness of their sockets in the bedrock. In the centre of the ring lie four stones which may have formed a 'cove' setting; a male burial was found next to them.

AVEBURY

The huge circle-henge of Avebury (Wiltshire) is one
of the greatest prehistoric sites in Europe. Its bank
was 5 m high and 427 m in diameter; the steep
internal ditch was quarried through the white
chalk to a depth of 9 m, though it has now silted
up to a large extent. Over 90 000 cubic metres of
chalk were removed; and it has been estimated that
the bank and ditch required 1.5 million man-hours
of labour: for example, 250 people working for over
twenty years.

Just inside the ditch is the outer circle of ninety-
eight huge, unshaped sarsen boulders, up to 4.4 m
high – the positions of missing stones are now
marked with concrete blocks. This circle, by far the
biggest in Britain, enclosed two smaller rings. Since
one of these had a 'cove' of sarsens at its centre,
and the other a single pillar, they have inevitably
received 'female' and 'male' interpretations.

An avenue of one hundred pairs of sarsens ran
sinuously from the site to the 'Sanctuary' at
Overton Hill, 2.4 km away; each pair comprised a
tall, narrow stone and a broad, squatter stone –
another feature which has had a sexual
interpretation. The Avebury complex probably
dates to the late third millennium BC.

BARBURY CASTLE

Located by the Ridgeway, on the edge of the
Marlborough Downs, the impressive egg-shaped
hillfort of Barbury Castle (Wiltshire) has two strong
banks and deep ditches. Traces of hut foundations
and storage pits inside the fort have been seen from
the air, and Iron Age jewellery and chariot fittings
have been found here.

CALLANISH

On a promontory in Loch Roag on the island of Lewis (Western Isles) stands Callanish, the 'Stonehenge of the North', an important and complex site. The main feature consists of a ring, 13 m across, of thirteen tall slabs of the easily split Lewis gneiss; one stone, over 4.5 m high, stands at the centre. Between this and the eastern edge of the circle is a chambered round cairn of the Neolithic Age, the smallest in Britain.

The stones – none of them artificially shaped – are not enormous: even the central one weighs no more than 5 tons, and a mere twenty people could have hauled and erected it. An avenue of two rows of tall stones leads northward, with single rows running in the other three main directions, with the result that the monument as a whole is cross-shaped.

There have been many claims for astronomical alignments at Callanish, but a recent analysis found that all of them were unsatisfactory or could be due to chance. There are also many legends connected with the site: until the last century couples would often go there to make their marital vows, and there is even a superstition that a marriage would be very happy if it was first consummated among the stones! Another tale has it that the slabs are local giants who were turned to stone by St Kieran because they refused to be christened.

CASTLERIGG

The Carles or Castlerigg stone circle, in Cumbria, has a dramatic natural setting, and may be one of the earliest circles in Britain. It is a pear-shaped ring, 30 m across, comprising thirty-eight stones, most of them less than 1.5 m in height. There are also traces of a surrounding bank. A strange rectangle of ten stones stands inside the ring and adjoining its eastern arc.

CERNE ABBAS

The unique chalk-cut figure of the Cerne Abbas giant, 55 m long, is said to have been traced around the body of a real giant killed on this Dorset hillside! Its date is uncertain, but the club, almost 37 m long, makes it seem likely to be a representation of Hercules, perhaps dating to the second century AD, when worship of this god was revived. The genitalia are conspicuous – indeed the erect phallus has grown by over 1.5 m since the eighteenth century through the incorporation of the navel – and may therefore indicate some sort of fertility cult. Until recently, maypole dancing took place near the figure on May Day. It is said that women wishing to conceive would spend the night on the figure. The giant is still scoured every seven years.

DEVIL'S ARROWS

Three great stones, the Devil's Arrows in Yorkshire, each probably weathered rather than carved into the fluted shape seen at the top, stand in an almost straight line. The biggest is nearly 7 m high, with a further 2 m in the socket. They are of millstone grit, and were brought from a source over 10 km away. There used to be four or even five stones, in a line, but one of them was demolished in a fruitless search for treasure, and removed to form a bridge over a stream. On Midsummer's Day the fair of St Barnabas was held near here until the eighteenth century. The stones derive their name from a legend that the devil tried to destroy an early Christian settlement in the vicinity by firing arrows at it!

DULOE

The small stone circle of Duloe, in Cornwall, is located in the centre of the village; unlike all other Cornish circles and chambered tombs, which are made of granite, its large stones are of quartz, set in an oval ring, over 11 m across. Seven big upright slabs (the tallest nearly 3 m) and one reclining stone survive of this probably Bronze Age monument (late third millennium BC).

DUN CARLOWAY

On this rocky knoll in Lewis (Western Isles) stands
Dun Carloway, one of the best preserved brochs –
these uniquely Scottish structures are Iron Age
round towers of drystone masonry. This one is still
up to 9 m high, and has a double wall housing a
series of galleries linked by an intramural staircase.
The main door has a guardroom in the wall.

THE HURLERS

The Cornish Bronze Age monument known as The
Hurlers derives its name from a legend that the
slabs are men turned to stone for hurling a ball on
the Lord's Day. It comprises a trio of circles of
upright granite slabs; the circles lie, almost
touching, in a line on Bodmin Moor. The stones
were originally carefully shaped and set up with
their tops more or less level. There are two other
standing stones and over twenty round barrows in
the vicinity.

KNOWLTON

At Knowlton in Dorset, three henges – each a circular bank with an internal ditch – lie in an almost straight line. Two of them can now only be seen from the air, but this, the central henge, is still clearly visible at ground level. Almost 100 m in diameter, its bank is still quite high in places; the site is particularly notable for containing this twelfth-century church at its centre, an indication of an attempt at Christianisation of enduring beliefs associated with this Neolithic site.

LANYON QUOIT

The Neolithic tomb of Lanyon Quoit in Cornwall has now lost its covering mound, but three of its upright stones survive, restored in 1824 after a violent storm in 1815 made the chamber collapse. Owing to a legend that a giant's bones were found in it, the monument is also called Giant's Quoit or Giant's Table. In the distance can be seen the ruins of a tin mine.

LONG STONE

Close to Gatcombe Lodge chambered tomb in Gloucestershire stands the Long Stone, a roughly triangular slab of oolite, 2.3 m high, on top of a very slight mound. Thought to date to the fourth millennium BC, it may represent the remains of another burial chamber. The holes were caused by weathering, but led to a number of superstitions: for example, mothers used to put their babies through the holes in the hope of curing whooping cough or warding off rickets. There is also a tradition that when the Minchinhampton clock strikes midnight the stone runs around the field!

LONG HOUSE

The Long House chambered tomb, or 'Samson's Stone' (Carreg Samson), has a superb location overlooking the Dyfed coast, and was used as a shelter for sheep in the early years of this century. Its polygonal chamber has seven upright stones, although the great capstone (4.5 by 2.7 m) rests on only three of them.

MAIDEN CASTLE

Maiden Castle hillfort in Dorset is one of the biggest
and most impressive sites in Britain, with an inner
circumference of 2.5 km and mountainous
ramparts enclosing 18 hectares. There was
occupation on this site from Neolithic times
onward, but the great Iron Age defences seen here
were built around 150 BC and strengthened
c. 75 BC when Maiden Castle became a flourishing
town with a population of at least 1000 and with
far-flung trading contacts. Recent excavations have
revealed the foundations of three circular houses,
of *c.* 200 BC, with stone ovens and paved entrance
porches, as well as a series of huge storage pits for
grain. Geomagnetic survey shows that almost the
entire hilltop is covered by such foundations and
pits.

In AD 43 it was attacked and taken by the 2nd
Legion under Vespasian: a war cemetery has been
found outside one gate. By AD 70 the Britons had
been resettled in nearby Dorchester, and the fort
was deserted until, a few centuries later, a small
Romano-Celtic temple was built inside it.

MERRY MAIDENS

The Bronze Age monument of the Merry Maidens owes its name – like its Cornish name *Dans Maen*, 'stone dance' – to a story that the nineteen granite blocks are maidens turned to stone for dancing on a Sunday. They stand in a circle, almost 25 m across, and were shaped to make their tops level. As at many other circles there is also a legend that the stones cannot be moved – all attempts have failed, and the cattle used for the purpose fell down and died!

NINE STONES

The tiny circle of Nine Stones in a Dorset valley is
also known as the Devil's Nine Stones; Stukeley
thought it was a Celtic temple but in fact it dates
to the second millennium BC. The circle is 8.4 m in
diameter, and the irregularly spaced sarsens
comprise seven small and two large blocks – the
latter, 1.2 and 2.1 m high, stand on either side of
a low block at true north. The biggest stone weighs
no more than 8 tons. Inevitably, the circle is said
to be nine children turned to stone for playing
'Five-Stones' on a Sunday.

PENTRE IFAN

Pentre Ifan in Dyfed is a portal chamber whose enclosing cairn has now disappeared. Its three upright stones, 2.5 m in height, support a huge 17-ton capstone, 5 m in length.

RING OF BRODGAR

Located on a neck of land between the Loch of Stenness and Loch of Harray in the Orkneys, the Ring of Brodgar is not only the biggest and finest stone circle in Scotland but also one of the best and most complete in the whole of Britain. It is also, with Stenness (Pages 139–143), the most northerly circle-henge in the British Isles. The ditch, cut into rock, is 3 m deep, 9 m wide and 142 m in diameter; its bank is internal. This henge alone, therefore, would have required about 80 000 man-hours, or 100 labourers for three months.

The stone circle, 113 m across, still has twenty-seven of an original sixty stones; the tallest is 4.6 m in height. They are made of the local red sandstone which splits easily and naturally. It is possible that the site was once linked to Stenness by a line of stones, thus forming a complex like Avebury.

ROLLRIGHT STONES

Seventy-seven blocks of weathered limestone, the 'King's Men', form the circle known as the Rollright Stones on a ridge above the Oxford plain. They are a variety of shapes and sizes, and it is possible that they are fragments eroded from a smaller number of large stones. A prehistoric trackway led past the ring. The monument is thought to date to *c.* 2000 BC, and legend has it that the blocks are a king and his army (the 'King Stone' stands nearby) turned to stone by a witch. There is even a tale that infertile women can be cured by touching the stones with bare breasts! In the eighteenth century the local young people used to meet near the King Stone on Midsummer's Eve for dancing and feasting.

RUDSTON

The tallest standing stone in Britain is to be found at Rudston (Humberside) in the churchyard – another case of attempted Christianisation. Almost 8 m high, this 26-ton block of gritstone was hauled from a source on the coast 16 km away; it is thought to date to *c.* 2000 BC. The area also has three cursuses and two long barrows, and was thus of some importance in prehistory.

SCORHILL

The Devon stone circle of Scorhill, located by a stream, is one of the finest on Dartmoor. Estimates of its original total of granite stones range from thirty-six to seventy; twenty-three still stand, and a further seven or eight have fallen. They are mostly pointed in form, but have not been shaped or made level; the tallest is 2.4 m in height, and the circle is almost 27 m across. It probably dates to the Bronze Age.

SILBURY HILL

There have been many strange theories about Silbury Hill in Wiltshire, the biggest man-made prehistoric mound in Europe: for example, that it was a huge sundial, or the womb of a huge surface-depiction of the earth goddess. However, the most common belief has been that it contains a rich burial, and attempts have been made to locate this. In 1776 Cornish tin miners were employed to sink a shaft straight down from the top, but nothing was found; in 1849 a different approach was tried when a tunnel was dug from the base through to the centre, and side galleries were opened up, but once again without result. In the late 1960s, the BBC sponsored a new tunnel, dug in from the base. This work did not uncover a burial either, but it did show that the mound, comprising 354 000 cubic metres of chalk, was probably constructed in four phases. Plant remains from its core gave a radiocarbon date of 2145 BC – previously the only proof that the mound was prehistoric was the fact that a Roman road made a detour around its base. The mound is almost 40 m high, and it has been estimated that 18 million man-hours – i.e. 500 workers for ten years – were required in its construction.

SKARA BRAE

The 'British Pompeii' of Skara Brae in the Orkneys is a Neolithic village, built of stone owing to lack of timber, which survived by being buried in sand by a storm – its occupants must have departed hurriedly. It was another storm which, in 1850, uncovered the ruins of this, the best preserved Neolithic village in Europe.

The nine small, squarish huts, which probably had roofs of organic material, had walls over a metre in thickness. They were linked together by covered alleyways. As can be seen, inside the huts are well-built central hearths, stone furniture such as upright 'dressers', and beds on either side of the hearths. Cupboard-recesses are found in the walls, and privies are known.

The whole site was surrounded, sheltered and almost buried by its dump of ash, bone, shells and dung. The village, dating back to the mid-third millennium BC, probably housed seven or eight families, a total of thirty or forty people.

ST LYTHANS

The St Lythans (Maes y Felin) chambered long-barrow in Glamorgan is also known as Gwâl-y-Filiart, the greyhound bitch's kennel. It has three uprights of mudstone, and a huge capstone – which is said to whirl round three times on Midsummer's Eve, when the stones also go to bathe in the river! There is even a legend that the field in which the monument stands is cursed, and that the stones would grant wishes whispered to them on Hallowe'en. The rectangular chamber stood at the eastern end of a mound which was about 27 m long. Some human remains and coarse potsherds were found here.

STENNESS

The henge of Stenness (Orkneys) had a ditch dug
2 m into sandstone: 1200 tons were removed,
which would have meant 100 people labouring for
three months. The external bank is 61 m in
diameter. The stone circle of tall unshaped local
flagstones – perhaps quarried from the ditch –
originally comprised twelve blocks, of which four
survive. The ring was 31 m across. The site dates
to the late third millennium BC, and may have been
linked to the Ring of Brodgar (Pages 103–113) by
an avenue. In the eighteenth century Stenness was
known as the Temple of the Moon, Brodgar as that
of the Sun. Dances and feasts took place here on
New Year's Day.

STONEHENGE

The unique monument of Stonehenge, on Salisbury Plain in Wiltshire, was built and modified over the course of 700 years in the late third and early second millennia BC. It began as a simple henge – a circular bank, almost 2 m high, an external quarry ditch, and a small external bank. Subsequently, eighty blocks of diorite, the 'bluestones', were brought by land and water from the Preseli Hills (Dyfed) – 217 km as the crow flies – and set up inside the earthworks in two concentric circles. An 'avenue' of parallel banks and external ditches ran from the Avon up to the site's entrance, possibly the route by which the bluestones were brought to the site.

Finally, eighty huge sarsens from the Marlborough Downs were brought 32 km to the site; since they weigh from 20 to 50 tons, it probably took 1000 men seven weeks to transport each of them, a total of ten years' work. The bluestone circles were dismantled; the sarsens were shaped and set up in a ring as a series of thirty uprights (about 26 tons each) with tenons projecting at the top; then a series of level lintels, with mortices on their underside (see Page 151), were set above them, interlocking and curved to form a circle. An inner horseshoe of five 'trilithons' – each of two uprights with a single lintel – rose to 6 or 7 m in height, but only two of these now survive intact. Some of the bluestones were set up inside the horseshoe, and others formed a circle around it.

The dagger and axe carvings on one of the inner sarsens (Page 13) led some scholars to postulate a link with Mycenae; recent radiocarbon dates have upheld this possibility. Stonehenge was probably aligned on the midsummer sunrise, but other claims for more complex astronomical alignments are much more doubtful. It was clearly a major centre of some kind, and is surrounded by many barrow cemeteries, including some spectacularly rich burials, as well as a cursus monument. Apart from its imaginary links with Druids the site also has several legends associating it with Merlin.

SWINSIDE

The Cumbrian circle of Swinside on the open fells
is a superb, compact setting of fifty-five blocks of the
local grey slate, forming a ring 27 m in diameter.
Originally the stones would have been almost
touching all the way around except at the fine
double portal. Excavation has shown that they
were set up on a bed of rammed pebbles. This
Bronze Age site is also called 'Sunken Kirke'
through a legend according to which the stones
were supposed to be used for the construction of a
church, but the devil caused them to sink into the
ground.

TRETHEVY QUOIT

Trethevy Quoit in Cornwall is a most impressive Neolithic portal chamber, also known as the Giant's House. It has lost its covering mound since the last century, but the great chamber, almost 5 m in height, survives. There are seven uprights, a massive capstone nearly 4 m long with a hole through it, and a cross-stone dividing the chamber: it can be seen that a corner fragment was broken off to allow a body to be inserted.

UFFINGTON

The Uffington hillfort, located near the hill-figure (Page 171) in Oxfordshire, probably dates to the Iron Age, and has two impressive chalk-rubble banks with a ditch in between. The inner bank had a facing of sarsen stones. In this photograph one can see the bank and ditch at the north side.

UFFINGTON

The great hill-figure at Uffington, 110 by 40 m, was made by stripping away the turf to expose the chalk beneath; it is best seen from a distance or from the air. It may represent a dragon, because the flat hill in the valley below (shown on page 171 seen from the figure's ear) is called Dragon Hill – there is a story that St George killed the dragon on it, and the patch where nothing grows was where the blood spilled! However, it is far more likely that the figure is a horse; since it resembles depictions on Iron Age coins, it is thought to date to that period, like the nearby fort. Thus it might be the tribal emblem of the Dobunni or the Atrebates, although some scholars believe it might have been made in early Anglo-Saxon times, or to celebrate Alfred's victory over the Danes in AD 871. The earliest known record of the figure dates to the eleventh century. Since then, it has been scoured every seven years, an occasion which used to witness festivities and sports in the fort. Inevitably the figure is associated with many legends: for example, making a wish while standing on the eye is supposed to be lucky!

The photograph on page 173 is the view west towards the 'Manger' from below the horse.

WAYLAND'S SMITHY

A great burial mound, now standing in a beech
grove near the Ridgeway in Oxfordshire,
Wayland's Smithy derives its name from Volund
the Smith, a northern god who is said to have made
the shoes for the nearby Uffington horse
(Page 171). There is a tale that if a traveller's horse
lost a shoe, he could leave the animal by the tomb
and place a coin on a stone; when he returned the
money would have disappeared and the horse
would be shod! The wedge-shaped mound of earth
was set up *c.* 2820 BC on top of an earlier, smaller
mound and wooden mortuary structure containing
fourteen bodies. The impressive façade (Page 177)
at the southern end still has four huge sarsen
stones, 3 m high; the passage led to an
antechamber and a cross-shaped burial chamber
housing eight bodies.

WEST KENNET

One of the largest Neolithic mounds in Britain, the great wedge-shaped structure of the West Kennet long-barrow in Wiltshire is over 100 m in length. At its eastern end is the great façade of upright sarsen stones in front of a concave forecourt. A passage leads into the mound, with two small chambers on either side. A seventeenth-century doctor dug up bones here for use as medicine. Excavators in 1956 found remains of forty-six people of all ages; all the adults over thirty had arthritis; and a variety of other ailments, abscesses and fractures could be seen in the remains, which were found disarticulated in the side chambers, together with pottery and flints. After being in use for about 1000 years, the tomb was filled with earth, and its entrance blocked with the huge slabs.